Second Edition
Pawz Publishing, LLC

Cover design by Kurt Zendzian

Written and illustrated by Rebekah Phillips
www.rebekahphillips.com
Contact: info@farleeandfriends.com

Edited by Christine DeOrio

Library of Congress #TXu-002093039

ISBN 978-0-9861309-3-9

Printed in China

Special thanks to Dre London for your inspiring ideas and for helping to make this book possible; to Cristina Bohorquez for your helpful guidance; to my husband Kurt for your love and support, design talent, and daily motivation; and to my family and childhood friends who have helped to shape these stories with fond memories.

www.farleeandfriends.com

FaRLee

Farlee
and friends
The Perfect Gift

by Rebekah Phillips

Pawz Publishing, LLC

Farlee H. Hawkins woke up from his afternoon nap. He didn't like to take naps, but he wanted to grow tall like his papa and be strong like his Uncle Norman, so he always took his nap. This afternoon, it had been hard for him to rest with all the noise. Christmas was only one day away, and the house was full of guests. Farlee listened to the sound of joyful conversations coming from downstairs. It seemed like everyone was feeling happy, except for him.

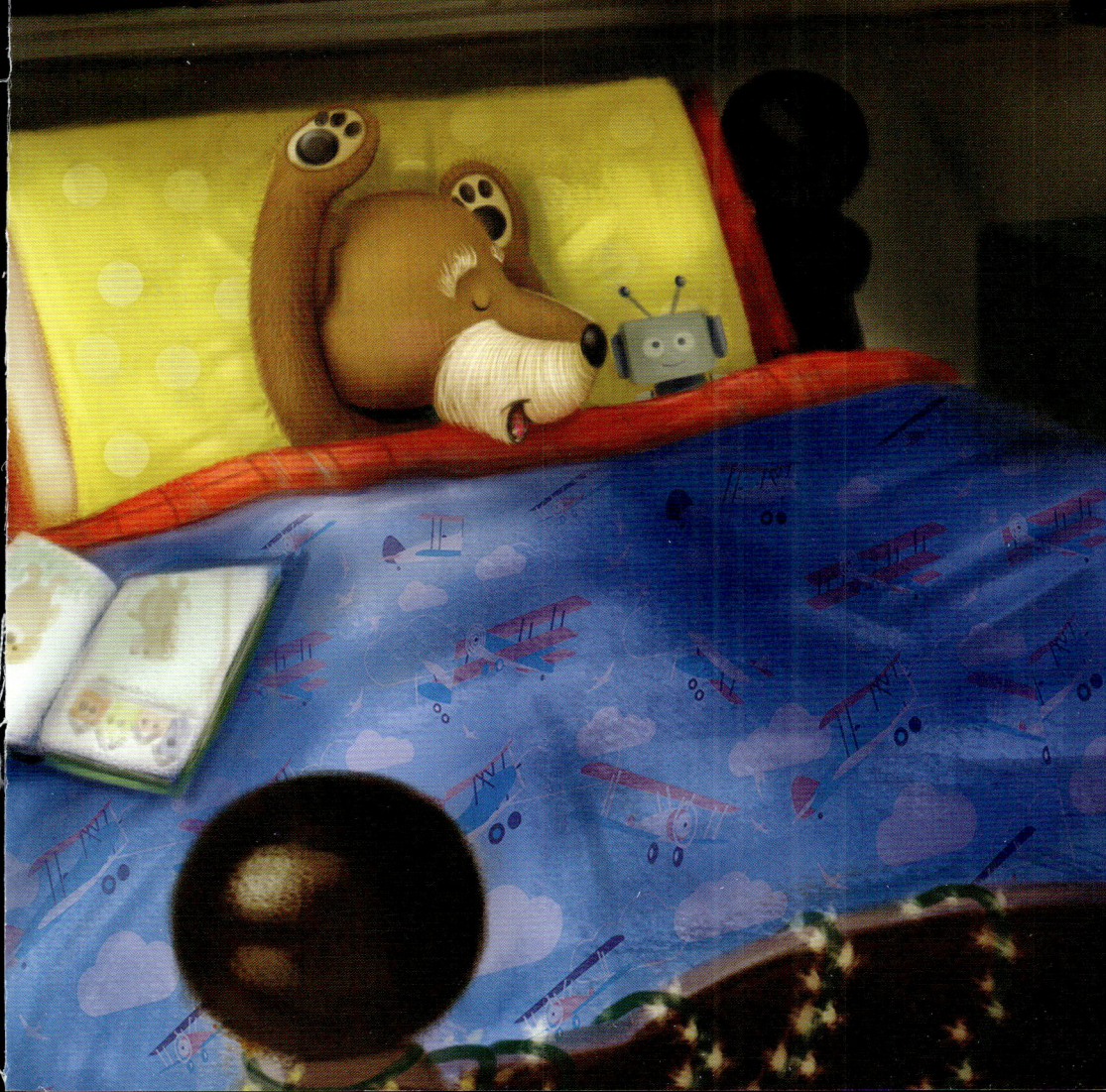

Farlee had been thinking all week long about what he would give his mom for Christmas, and he still didn't have an idea. It had to be a special gift! He wanted her to know just how much he loved her. Now that he felt rested from his nap, he could think of something. He took out some paper and crayons and started to draw. A robot? A car? A picture of mom? But no, no, no, nothing came out right. He switched from crayons to markers and tried again: An airplane? Some flowers? A picture of their house? But nothing seemed good enough to be the perfect gift.

"Maybe I'll go outside to think," Farlee said to himself.

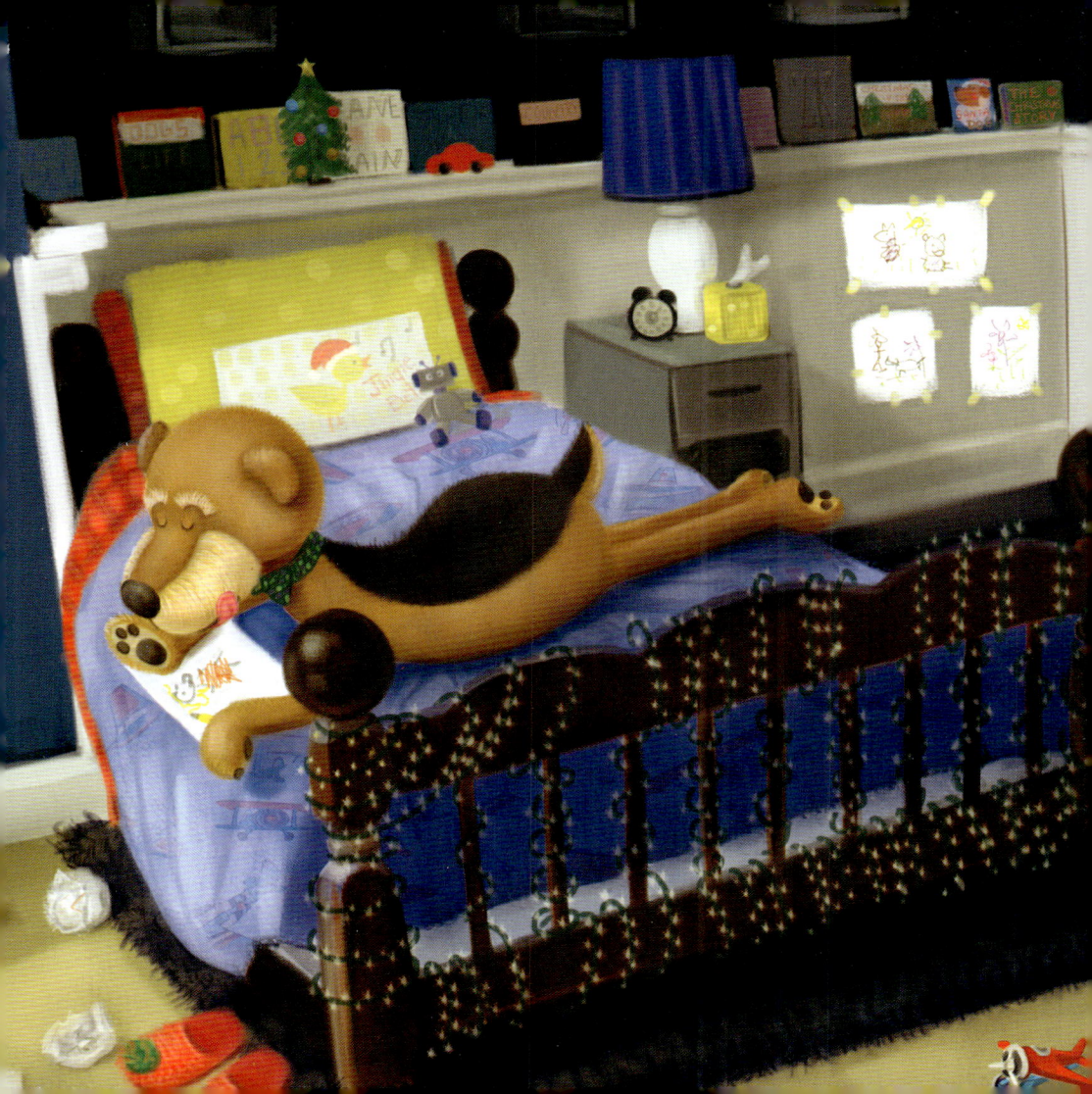

Farlee whistled as he thumped loudly down the stairs, then he squeezed past Uncle Norman and Aunt Peggy to reach the coat closet. He put on his favorite red boots and puffy red coat, then peeked around the corner for his friend, Cornelius.

Cornelius was a field mouse who lived under the stairs. The two of them had a secret code: When Cornelius heard Farlee whistle, he knew it was safe to sneak out from his mouse hole. No one else in the family knew about Cornelius—so Farlee hid him in his coat pocket.

Cornelius would know what to do. He always had great ideas!

Outside, the snow looked magical as it danced in the wind, but it felt cold on Farlee's nose.

"Cornelius, are you warm enough in there?" Farlee asked as he looked into his pocket. "Yes!" Cornelius squeaked. "Quite warm indeed!" (He was a very proper mouse.)

"I don't know what to do," Farlee sighed. "Christmas is tomorrow, and I need to make the perfect gift for my mom."

"Let's do a 'thinking' walk!" Cornelius said.

Farlee and Cornelius began to march around the yard, creating a pattern of footsteps in the freshly fallen snow.

Cornelius started to suggest ideas:

"What if you sing your mom a Christmas song?"

"I don't know," Farlee said. "Singing makes me feel shy. I don't want to mess it up."

"What about a hat made out of branches?" Cornelius said.

"I don't think it will be very warm," Farlee replied.

After their third walk around the yard, Cornelius squeaked excitedly, "What about a snow-dog?"

"YES! That's it! Great idea, Cornelius!" Farlee exclaimed. "We can make a beautiful snow-dog that looks just like my mom! It will be the perfect gift!

"I think we will need to get some of her things to dress the snow-dog," Farlee added. "I'll begin to roll up the snow, and you sneak into the house and get my mom's winter hat and scarf."

"OK!" Cornelius squeaked. He would have to be very careful to not be seen.

They worked for the rest of the afternoon building the snow-dog. It had arms and a tail made from fallen branches, and brown leaves for ears, but best of all, the snow-dog was wearing Farlee's mom's very own hat and scarf.
It looked just like her!

"It's perfect!" Farlee exclaimed.
"It's a masterpiece!" Cornelius squeaked.
"But how will we get it under the Christmas tree?"

"Let's wrap it up in wrapping paper and wheel it
into the garage on my brother's skateboard," Farlee said.
"Then we can sneak it into the house
once everyone is asleep."

Farlee was proud of himself for coming up
with such a smart plan.

His mom was going to be so surprised
when she saw his perfect gift!

After a cup of hot cocoa and a nice warm bath, Farlee could hardly wait for everyone to go to bed. The entire family sat in the living room talking, laughing, and enjoying the sound of crackling logs from the fireplace. They decided they would each open one present from Grandma tonight, and save the rest for the morning. Farlee looked around at all the wrapped packages under the tree. He was certain that no other present would be as special as his gift for his mom.

Farlee and his brother opened their presents from Grandma: Christmas pajamas, a Hawkins family tradition! Tomorrow morning, they would all meet downstairs wearing their matching pj's, and Grandpa would read *The Christmas Story*. Then they would open their presents from family and Santa. Farlee was so excited!

"Goodnight, Cornelius," Farlee whispered toward the mouse hole as he headed up the stairs. "I'll meet you by the garage once everyone is asleep to sneak our snow-dog under the tree." "OK!" Cornelius squeaked as quietly as he could. He would try his best to stay awake.

Later that night, guided by the light from the moon, Farlee and Cornelius snuck out to the garage and wheeled in the snow-dog. Squeak, squeak, thump! The skateboard was making a lot of noise, but fortunately, no one woke up.

"I'm so excited!" Farlee whispered. "I'm more excited to see my mom open the beautiful snow-dog than I am to get my gifts from Santa!" "Really?" Cornelius squeaked. "You MUST be excited! I can't wait to see what Santa brought for me!"

The next morning, the sun shone brightly through the window into Farlee's bedroom, and the smell of pancakes wafted past his nose. He leapt out of bed, put on his fuzzy slippers, and ran downstairs. "Cornelius, wake up! It's Christmas!" Farlee said excitedly. Cornelius ran out of his mouse hole and jumped into Farlee's pajama shirt pocket. They both couldn't wait to see Farlee's mom's face when she opened the snow-dog.

There was a lot of commotion in the living room.

"Why is the floor soaking wet?" Farlee's dad yelled. "Why is my skateboard in here?" Farlee's brother shouted. "We must have a leak in the roof!" Farlee's mom gasped.

Farlee saw the skateboard covered with wet wrapping paper. He saw a giant puddle of water that threatened the pile of wrapped presents under the tree. His heart sank.

The beautiful snow-dog had melted.

Farlee felt warm tears running down his cheeks as he slumped down on the sofa. Cornelius let out little whimpers from Farlee's pocket. In between sobs, Farlee told his mom that he had made her the most beautiful snow-dog. "I just wanted to make you the perfect gift," he explained, "but instead, I've made a great big mess. I didn't know it would melt—and now I've ruined Christmas!" Farlee's older brother was holding in a laugh, but then everyone started to giggle. Farlee didn't think it was funny at all.

"Oh, Farlee," his mom said, smiling gently as she gave him a great big hug. "You didn't know the snow-dog would melt. I'm sure it was beautiful! How about after we clean this up and open our presents, we build another snow-dog together? This time, we will keep her outside where she won't melt."

Farlee smiled between tears. "OK, Mom. I'm glad you aren't mad at me."

"How could I be mad?" his mom asked. "It's the precious thought that counts. On Christmas Day and every day, it's the thought that matters most."

Later that afternoon, as the sun glistened on the snow, Farlee and his mom made another beautiful snow-dog. Then Grandma took a picture of Farlee and his mom together in front of it. "Farlee, you know what I'm going to do?" his mom asked. "I'm going to frame this picture and hang it up on my special memory wall in the office, so we can remember the snow-dog forever."

"Great idea, Mom!" Farlee said. "Maybe the snow-dog was the perfect gift after all!"

"YOU are my perfect gift, Farlee," his mom said as she hugged him tightly. "You are mine too, Mom," Farlee said.

As the sun began to set, snowflakes floated gently down from the sky. The chill of the evening air seemed to go right through their jackets. "I think it's time we say goodbye to the snow-dog, and head inside for some dinner," Farlee's mom said. So Farlee and his mom trudged their way through the snow, back toward the warmth of the house. Cornelius let out a squeaky yawn from his hiding place.

"Farlee?"

"Yes, Mom?"

"What is that in your coat pocket?"